Cambridge **Discovery Education™**

► **INTERACTIVE READERS**

Series editor: Bob Hastings

PARIS
CITY OF LIGHT

A1

Simon Beaver

CAMBRIDGE
UNIVERSITY PRESS

Discovery
EDUCATION

CAMBRIDGE UNIVERSITY PRESS
Cambridge, New York, Melbourne, Madrid, Cape Town,
Singapore, São Paulo, Delhi, Mexico City

Cambridge University Press
32 Avenue of the Americas, New York, NY 10013-2473, USA

www.cambridge.org
Information on this title: www.cambridge.org/9781107645776

First published 2014

Printed in Hong Kong, China, by Golden Cup Printing Company Limited

A catalog record for this publication is available from the British Library.

Library of Congress Cataloging-in-Publication Data

Beaver, Simon.
  Paris : city of light / Simon Beaver.
      pages cm. -- (Cambridge discovery interactive readers)
   ISBN 978-1-107-64577-6 (pbk. : alk. paper)
1. Paris (France)--Juvenile literature. 2. English language--Textbooks for foreign speakers.
3. Readers (Elementary) I. Title.

CB311.H328 2014
930--dc23

2013025114

ISBN 978-1-107-64577-6

Additional resources for this publication at www.cambridge.org

Layout services, art direction, book design, and photo research: Q2ABillSMITH GROUP
Editorial services: Hyphen S.A.
Audio production: CityVox, New York
Video production: Q2ABillSMITH GROUP

Contents

Before You Read: Get Ready!

Paris is one of the most beautiful and interesting cities in the world.

Words to Know

Look at the pictures. Then complete the sentences below with the correct words.

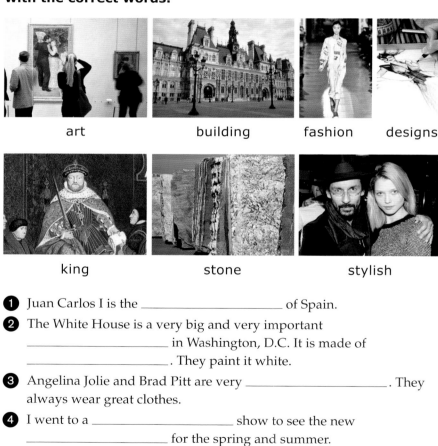

art   building   fashion   designs

king   stone   stylish

1 Juan Carlos I is the _____ of Spain.

2 The White House is a very big and very important _____ in Washington, D.C. It is made of _____. They paint it white.

3 Angelina Jolie and Brad Pitt are very _____. They always wear great clothes.

4 I went to a _____ show to see the new _____ for the spring and summer.

5 I love Picasso's _____. He was a great painter.

Words to Know

Read the text. Then complete the sentences below with the correct highlighted words.

Why do so many tourists visit Paris?

Architecture: the buildings and the bridges over the river Seine are beautiful.

Culture: the movies, food, and art museums are great.

1. Dolores is studying _____. She wants to make beautiful buildings.

2. In the summer, there are a lot of _____ in Paris. It's difficult to walk around!

3. Boats on the river go under many _____.

4. The Louvre is one of the many great art _____ in Paris.

5. Paris is a city of _____ , with great writers, movie-makers, fashion designers, and artists.

Comparatives

Complete the sentences with words from the box.

tall	taller (than)	(the) tallest
good	better (than)	(the) best
famous	more famous (than)	(the) most famous

The Eiffel Tower is the ❶ _____ building in Paris. It has more than 18,000 visitors a day. It is also the
❷ _____ building in the city. It is 228 meters
❸ _____ than Big Ben in London. It's the
❹ _____ place to look at Paris!

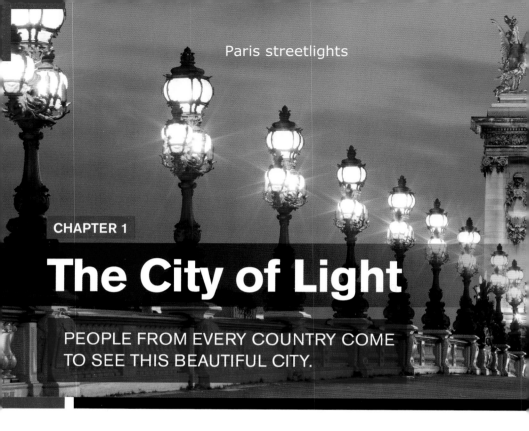

Paris streetlights

CHAPTER 1

The City of Light

PEOPLE FROM EVERY COUNTRY COME TO SEE THIS BEAUTIFUL CITY.

Paris – the City of Light. But why is it called that? One answer is that Paris was one of the first cities in Europe to have streetlights (in 1828). But another answer is that 300 years ago many great philosophers[1] lived in Paris. Their ideas[2] brought light to people's thinking and changed the world.

Paris is the world's favorite city for tourists. About 42 million people visit every year! There are beautiful hotels and great restaurants – French cooking is also famous. And there's so much to see: the Eiffel Tower, the Louvre Museum, Notre Dame!

[1]**philosopher:** a teacher and thinker
[2]**ideas:** new, different thinking

About 12 million people live in the Paris region,[3] but only 2.2 million live inside the old city walls. One hundred years ago, there were many factories and workers' homes in Paris. But now, homes are very expensive in the city. In the cheapest part of Paris, you can pay $300,000 for only two rooms!

Paris is also a very important place for **business**. A quarter of all the money in France comes from the Paris region. Many world businesses have buildings in Paris, too.

....

[3] **Paris region:** Paris and places around it

A six-room home in Invalides, Paris: $3.8 million

Businesses in La Défense, near the city

Video Quest

Paris

Watch the video about things to do in Paris. How do visitors get into the Louvre Museum?

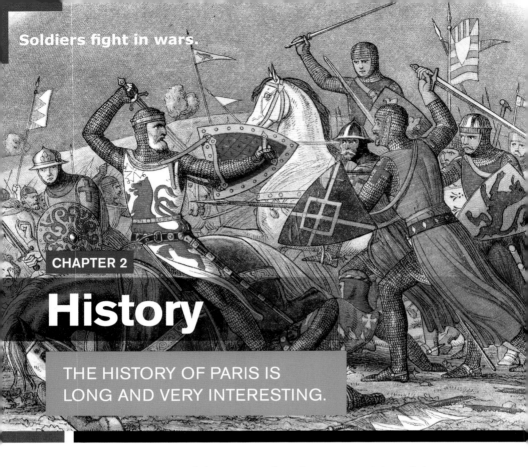

Soldiers fight in wars.

CHAPTER 2

History

THE HISTORY OF PARIS IS
LONG AND VERY INTERESTING.

Paris is a very old city with a long, exciting **history**. There were villages in the region 6,000 years ago. Then the Romans came 2,000 years ago. They built a town called *Lutetia Parisiorum*.

In 1348, there were 200,000 Parisians.[4] That was a lot. Only 50,000 people lived in London then.

For **centuries**, there were many wars in France. Most people were poor and hungry. In the 17th century, the poor people of Paris got **angry**. They started fighting the king, Louis XIV.

....

[4]**Parisians:** people of Paris

8

In 1648, the king took his family and all the most important people in France to Versailles, 20 kilometers from Paris. There, they lived in a very big palace. They felt safe from the poor people.

Louis XIV was king for 72 years! In that time Paris got smaller and less important, and Versailles got bigger and more expensive. In the end, Louis's palace took about 30 percent of all the money in France! The poor people of France got very angry.

? ANALYZE

Why do you think the poor people got angry?

The Palace of Versailles

Paris, 1789: Parisians storm the Bastille.

The 17th and 18th centuries were the time of the Enlightenment. Great philosophers and writers in Paris wanted change. They wanted a better world that was good for everybody, not only the king and his friends.

On July 14, 1789, angry people stormed an important building, the Bastille, in Paris. This was the beginning of the French **Revolution**. At first, the people tried to talk with the king, Louis XVI, but he didn't listen. So, in January 1793, the French guillotined him in Paris. A few months later, his wife, Marie Antoinette, also died on the guillotine.

Now there are no kings in Versailles, and Paris is the **capital** of the Republic of France.

In 1940, Nazi soldiers came to Paris. It was a very bad time. There wasn't much food, and people weren't safe.

Nazi soldiers in World War II

Then in 1944, the Allies – French, American, British, and other soldiers – fought the Nazis for Paris. Dietrich von Choltitz was the most important German soldier in Paris. Hitler told him to blow up the city before the Allies got there. But he didn't. He said it was too beautiful. So Paris still has its beautiful buildings today.

The history of Paris is very interesting. Why not learn more about it?

In a war, soldiers sometimes blow up buildings or whole cities.

CHAPTER 3

Architecture

WHY IS PARIS SO BEAUTIFUL?

Paris has a special look. The architecture is the same in many places in the city.

About 150 years ago, most streets and buildings in Paris were very old. The streets weren't very clean. And they were very narrow. It was difficult for many people to walk through them at one time.

So the last French king, Napoleon III, asked a man named Georges-Eugène Haussmann to build a new Paris. Haussmann made wide streets and built beautiful new stone buildings, all with the same architecture. That's why Paris is so beautiful!

Haussmann built wide streets.

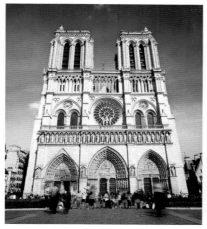

Notre Dame

Champs-Élysées, July 14

Today, thanks to Haussmann, Paris has many wide streets, called avenues and boulevards. There are also a lot of beautiful parks, museums, churches like Notre Dame, and old bridges like the Pont Neuf.

The famous Champs-Élysées Avenue is beautiful. It has many stores – and some very expensive restaurants and cafés! On July 14 each year, many people go there to watch French soldiers and planes going down the avenue from the Arc de Triomphe to the Tuileries **gardens**.

Video Quest

Paris Bridges

Watch the video about bridges in Paris. Why did King Henry build a new bridge?

The most famous building in Paris isn't really a building at all. It's the Eiffel Tower.

Gustave Eiffel built his famous tower in 1889, 100 years after the Revolution. It is very tall: 324 meters. Tourists love to go up the tower and see Paris from above.

The Eiffel Tower is unusual because most buildings in Paris aren't very tall. In 1973, work ended on the Montparnasse Tower. It was a new kind of building, 210 meters tall. Most Parisians didn't like it. So new buildings in Paris can't be so tall now.

The Eiffel Tower and Montparnasse

Pompidou Center

Paris has some interesting new buildings, too.

In the 1970s, the French **government** built an exciting new building – the Pompidou Center. Inside are a museum of modern art, a big library,[5] and a place for studying music. Millions of people visit it.

Another beautiful new building is the Bastille Opera. Paris now has two opera houses – an old one and a new one. Some of the world's best singers come to sing in Paris. Beautiful music for a beautiful city!

[5]**library:** People go to a library to find interesting books.

 APPLY

What's the architecture like in your country's capital?

CHAPTER 4

Culture

Dance at the Moulin de la Galette
Renoir, 1876

PARIS IS A CITY OF CULTURE, WITH ART, ARCHITECTURE, MOVIES, AND FASHION.

Paris is a very important place for culture. It has a long history of art and artists. Its museums show work by great French artists like Renoir, Rodin, and Cézanne – and other painters who came to live in Paris, like Van Gogh, Picasso, and Dalí.

A lot of writers also came from other countries to live in Paris. For example, in the 1920s, the American writers Ernest Hemingway, Gertrude Stein, and F. Scott Fitzgerald lived in Paris. Artists and writers often met in cafés like *Les Deux Magots* to talk about their ideas. You can visit the café today, too, but now it's very expensive!

France makes a lot of movies. A Frenchman, Louis Le Prince, "the father of film," made the world's first movie in 1888.

You can see Paris in many movies, too, for example *Amélie*, *The Bourne Identity*, and *The Da Vinci Code*. A great movie for seeing the city is Woody Allen's *Midnight in Paris*. It shows Paris today – and in the past. An American man from today goes back in time at midnight and meets all of the famous artists, writers, fashion designers, and beautiful people in Paris in the 1920s.

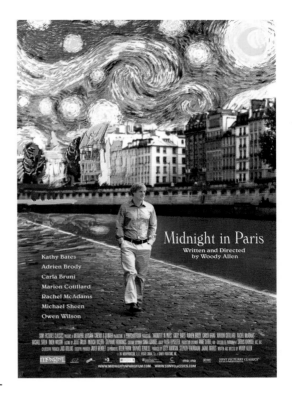

ANALYZE

Why do you think artists, writers, and filmmakers like Paris so much?

Chez Chartier

Night life is part of Paris culture. It's a city that gives you evenings to remember.

How about this? Walk down the river to the Marais, one of the oldest districts.[6] Visit the beautiful Place des Vosges there. It's a great place to live – if you can pay $1 million for two rooms!

Hungry? Paris has every kind of restaurant. Do you want French food? Dinner is $30 at Chez Chartier or $300 at La Tour d'Argent. You choose.

Later, why not end with a coffee in a stylish café in the Bastille district?

A great evening!

[6]**district:** part of a city

When you think of Paris, you think of fashion. Designer clothes from Yves St. Laurent or Pierre Cardin, bags from Hermès, but also perfume.

Paris has the greatest names in perfume, for example, Chanel, Givenchy, Lancôme, Cacharel, and Guerlain – one of the oldest perfume makers in France, nearly 200 years old. People pay billions of dollars every year for French perfume!

The real home of perfume isn't Paris. The businesses are there, but the factories are in the small town of Grasse, 700 kilometers from the capital. About 3,500 people make perfume there.

But the world wants "Chanel Paris" and not "Chanel Grasse"!

Chanel No. 5 is a very famous, and expensive, perfume.

Video Quest

Fashion

Watch the video about fashion in Paris. Why do you think designer clothing is so expensive?

The artists in Montmartre will draw your picture.

CHAPTER 5

What Do You Think?

NOW THAT YOU KNOW MORE ABOUT PARIS, IT'S TIME TO TAKE A VACATION THERE!

Imagine[7] you're going on vacation to Paris for a week. What five things do you most want to see and do? These can be things from this book or other things you know about Paris. There's a lot to choose from!

What time of year do you want to go to Paris? Why? And who do you want to go with?

Do you know French food? Do you want to eat French food in Paris? Or do you want food from another country? Paris has restaurants from nearly every country in the world. What food are you going to choose? Why?

[7]**imagine:** think about what something is like

And then there are souvenirs. What souvenirs do you want to bring home from France? What souvenirs are you going to buy for other people? Who?

Paris is the world's favorite place for tourists. What other five cities in the world do you most want to see after Paris? Why?

Enjoy traveling!

Souvenirs of Paris

After You Read

Choose Ⓐ (True) or Ⓑ (False). If the book does not tell you, choose Ⓒ (Doesn't say).

1 About 12 million people live inside the old walls of Paris.

- Ⓐ True
- Ⓑ False
- Ⓒ Doesn't say

2 Louis XIV went to live in the Palace of Versailles.

- Ⓐ True
- Ⓑ False
- Ⓒ Doesn't say

3 Haussmann made wider streets in Paris.

- Ⓐ True
- Ⓑ False
- Ⓒ Doesn't say

4 It's expensive to go to the opera in Paris.

- Ⓐ True
- Ⓑ False
- Ⓒ Doesn't say

5 Champs-Élysées Avenue is nearly two kilometers long.

- Ⓐ True
- Ⓑ False
- Ⓒ Doesn't say

6 The café Les Deux Magots is cheap today.

- Ⓐ True
- Ⓑ False
- Ⓒ Doesn't say

7 The first movie was made by a Frenchman.

(A) True

(B) False

(C) Doesn't say

8 Givenchy is the oldest perfume maker in France.

(A) True

(B) False

(C) Doesn't say

Looking at Cities

Write down three other cities. What country are they in?
How are they different from or like Paris?

City	Country	How it's different from or like Paris
1.		
2.		
3.		

Complete the Text

Use the words in the box to complete the paragraph.

built	narrow	stone	wide

Haussmann designed a new Paris. Before, many Paris streets were
1 _____ , but he made **2** _____
avenues. He also **3** _____ beautiful buildings made of
4 _____ .

Answer Key

Words to Know, page 4
1 king **2** building, stone **3** stylish **4** fashion, designs
5 art

Words to Know, page 5
1 architecture **2** tourists **3** bridges **4** museums
5 culture

Comparatives, page 5
1 most famous **2** tallest **3** taller **4** best

Video Quest, page 7
Visitors go under a pyramid to get into the Louvre.

Analyze, page 9
They were hungry and had no money, but the king had everything.

Video Quest, page 13
Because there was only one bridge in Paris, and too many people wanted to use it.

Apply, page 15 *Answers will vary.*

Analyze, page 17 *Answers will vary.*

Video Quest, page 19 *Answers will vary.*

True or False?, page 22
1 B **2** A **3** A **4** C **5** C **6** B **7** A **8** B

Looking at Cities, page 23 *Answers will vary.*

Complete the Text, page 23
1 narrow **2** wide **3** built **4** stone